Contents

The Survival Guide to Seriously Slippery Spellings

The Armadillo's Pillow Ltd

ISBN 978-1-912936-04-5

Cheltenham, United Kingdom

Introduction

Despite the wide availability of computerised spelling checkers in today's modern world, learning to spell is still an extremely important part of the educational process.

Spelling has long been a problem area for children, especially when encountering certain key words that seem to lie outside of the normal conventions – when phonics doesn't seem to work, and the old standard spelling rules are not applicable. Even when the rules do apply, it's easy to forget the rules and go with what looks right.

Homophones are another tricky challenge – you might remember that *stationary* and *stationery* are two different spellings, but may forget their meanings.

Add in the influence of foreign influences (American as well as others), the rise of texting and social media, and it is hard to keep up.

Utilising primarily mnemonics, visual cues, rhymes, and humorous drawings, *The Survival Guide to Seriously Slippery Spellings* attempts to tackle the trickiest words in a light-hearted yet effective way. For each word we have also identified the main definitions – the focus being on knowing the word, its main uses and how to spell it correctly.

This book contains over 250 words that we have found to be the most commonly misspelled. Surely there will be other words that your children find difficult to spell, but armed with these examples and strategies, they should be able to tackle other tricky spellings that they will encounter on their academic journey.

Funny drawings have been added to both encourage interest and aid in the educational process. Many studies have shown that visual aids not only increase the student's willingness to read, but increase comprehension. The humorous aspect of the pictures will inspire them to review the book again and again, thereby further ensuring the likelihood of spelling success.

Whilst the beginning targeted study age for this book is nine years, we feel that even older students, and maybe even a few parents, will benefit and have fun as well.

a lot *pronoun* - a large number or amount; *adverb* - a great deal, much

The word 'alot' **does not exist!** Remember a lot is two separate words.

You *can't use* <u>alittle</u> so you ***don't use*** <u>alot</u>!

allot *verb* - to give something, divide by share, for a particular purpose; to designate or put aside

Remember there are two *l*'s in allot.

I'm going to share these books with my children

That's a lot to **allot**.

absence *noun* - not being present; not existing

absen**t** becomes absen**ce**

*James had a **c**ommon **e**xcuse for his absen**ce** from school*

accelerate *verb* - make happen faster, to increase speed

*Two fast **c**ars (two **c**'s) in a**cc**elerate*

accept *verb* - agree to receive something; say yes to an invitation or offer; to consider something good or satisfactory

except *preposition, conjunction* - something not included; *verb* – specify as excluded from a group

These two words sound very similar

ac + cept = accept

*Please a**cc**ept this **c**razy **c**arpet (acc)*

ex + cept = except

*Nothing **exc**ept **ex**tra **c**are will save the planet (exc)*

accidentally *adverb* - by chance or mistake

Two c's and two l's in a**cc**identa**ll**y

*A **c**lose and **c**aring **all**y will help you in an a**cc**ident*

accommodate *verb* - provide with a place to live; to fit in with the needs of someone or something; assist

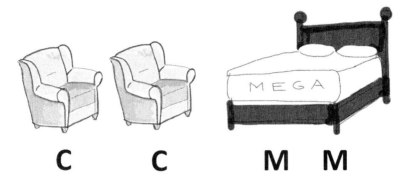

C   C   M   M

The a<u>cc</u>o<u>mm</u>odation had two <u>C</u>omfy
<u>C</u>hairs and a <u>M</u>ega <u>M</u>attress

accompany *verb* - go with someone as a companion

Don't forget the two *c's*

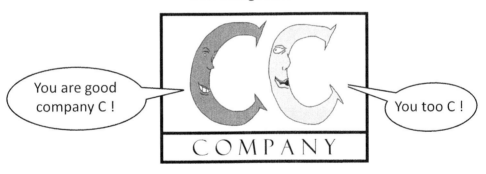

You are good company C !

You too C !

accurate *adjective* - correct in all details, exact

Remember that **accurate** also has two *c's*

Look twice to be certain. See (<u>C</u>) it twice

achieve
verb - succeed in a goal or aim, or to finish a difficult task

Achieve does follow the *i before e* rule, just remember that there <u>is</u> an *i*:

I ach**ie**ved with
<u>Eve</u>

Thanks
Eve!

acknowledge
verb - accept or admit the truth, or existence of something; to tell someone you have received something they sent

To acknowledge is to *KNOW*
ac**know**ledge

Did you bring
any pizza?

I **<u>know</u>** you're on the
<u>ledge</u>. That's why I
brought the ladder!

acquaintance
noun - someone you have met, but do not know well

The informally-used word *ain't* (contraction of am not, is not) can help

An acqua<u>int</u>ance
***<u>ain't</u>** a real friend*

acquire
verb - get or buy something

Don't forget the *c*

*I see (**c**) you wish to acquire the ice Cream*

advice
noun - an opinion or recommendation offered to help you

Advice is encouragement

Don't confuse with advise

ADVI**CE** = noun
ADVI**SE** = verb

FREE ADVICE
LEMONADE £1

aerial
adjective - happening in the air;   *noun* - a TV antenna

Don't forget the *e*

It's not aerial without an E!

affect *verb*	**effect** *noun*
to make a difference to something	a change which is the result of an action

Affect = ACTION

Effect = Change

RAVEN =
Remember Affect is a Verb, Effect is a Noun

use the raven to remember

*********** more on effect (use as a NOUN) ***********

An **effect** can also be an image or sound used in a play, television show or movie	An **effect** can also be a personal item or belonging
'The movie had some great special effects.'	*'Before departing the train you should make sure you haven't forgotten any personal effects.'*

aggressive *adjective* - behaving in an intense, angry and possibly violent way; being forceful to get something or win

Don't forget that there are two g's and two s's in a**gg**re**ss**ive:

Two sides go to war – *G* and *S* want more

agreeable *adjective* - pleasant; accepted by everyone; willing to do or accept something

Agree • able

I am <u>able</u> to <u>agree</u> with you

all right *adjective* - satisfactory; good enough; neither good or bad

All right is the correct way to spell the informally-used *'alright'*

ALL   RIGHT

*It's all right when you keep it **all** separate.*
Right?

almost *adverb* - nearly

Remember there is only one *l* in almost:

Almost is not all

amateur *noun* - a beginner, not professional

amateur

a mate u r

(A mate you are)

ambiguous *adjective* - having more than one meaning; not clear

What is that?

I don't know, but it has a **BIG U!**

*There's a **BIG U** in am**bigu**ous*

among *preposition* - in the middle of, or surrounded by others; being included as part of a group

Among (or also amongst) is sometimes misspelled with a *u*

*A **mon**(k) was among them.*

analysis *noun* - the process of studying something in detail

Why does my analysis always have a **Y**?

I don't know wh**y**, **Sis**

Remember there is a *y* where you might expect an *I* in analysis.

anchor *noun* - a heavy weight that keeps a boat from floating away; someone or something that gives support when needed

*An an**ch**or is held by a **ch**ain **or** something else.*

ancient *adjective* - of or from a very long time ago

Ancient **N**ames **C**an **I**nspire **E**very **N**ew **T**ale

angle *noun* - a measurement of the intersection of two lines

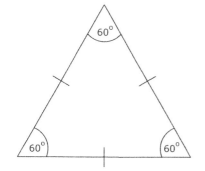

Don't confuse ang<u>le</u> with ang<u>el</u>:

Ang<u>les</u> **L**ie **E**verywhere

The ang<u>el</u> s<u>**ang**</u> **el**egantly

apparent *adjective* - clear

Key is to remember the two *p's* – think of an app

Can I have my phone back now Dad?

*Apparently the <u>parent</u> liked the <u>**app**</u>.*

10

appearance
noun - when someone is seen in public; the way a thing or person looks to others

ap • pear • ance

*__A p__ea and a __pear__
made an __appear__ance*

appreciate
verb - value or admire something highly

With appreciate , remember to use a *c* instead of *sh*

*She __appreciated__ the
__app__ and could see (__c__) it
was good.*

argument
noun - a disagreement

Remember to remove the *e* from argue for the correct spelling of *argument*

Eddie (__E__) left the argument

arithmetic *noun* - Study of mathematics (addition/subtraction/multiplication/division)

<u>A</u> <u>R</u>at <u>I</u>n <u>T</u>he <u>H</u>ouse <u>M</u>ay <u>E</u>at <u>T</u>he <u>I</u>ce <u>C</u>ream

ascend *verb* - to go up, or climb something; rise to a higher position

descend *verb* - to go down, or come down

It is easier to think about both words as they have similar spellings.

<u>Don't forget the C</u>

<u>C</u>limbers <u>a</u>scend, then <u>de</u>scend the mountain

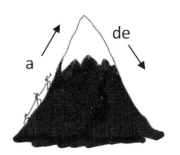

a

de

assassination *noun* - the murder of a prominent person

There are two sets of s's in assassination. You can use this phrase to keep that in mind:

An assassination is <u>s</u>omething <u>s</u>erious and <u>s</u>ometimes <u>s</u>topped.

Just stop it, Johnny!

attached *adjective* - joined, fastened or connected to something; full of affection

*The T's are a**tt**ached*

autumn *noun* - the season after summer and before winter

Key is not to forget the *n* at the end of the word.

Think of <u>N</u>ovember at the end of autum<u>n</u>

average *noun* - the mean of a selected range of numbers; a level that is considered to be typical or usual

Divide this word in two parts (ave • rage) and remember this phrase:

*(D)**ave** was in an average **rage***

awe   *noun* - a feeling of respect, wonder and fear

Remember the *e*...

Always **W**onderful and **E**xciting

awkward   *adjective* - difficult to deal with; causing problems, worry or embarrassment

*Two w's make this a**ww**kward*

Another W and we could be on the web

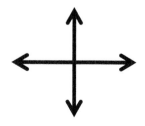

Awkward!

axis   *noun* - an imaginary line about which an object rotates; a fixed line on a graph used to show the position of a point

Don't put an *e* in axis!

*I use lines, not an ax**e**, to make an axis*

baffle *verb* - to cause someone to be unable to understand or explain something

Try to remember the double *-ff* and *-le* ending, like **WAFFLE**.

*The scientist was **baffle**d by the giant w**affle***

bargain *noun* - something at a lower price than its true value; an agreement made between two people or groups

*It's not a b**a**rg**a**in without two a's!*

The most common mistake is to forget the final *a*.

basically *adverb* - referring to the main or most important characteristic or feature

Try to remember there are two l's forming the word *all* after *basic*

*Basic**all**y you need them **ALL***

beautiful *adjective* - very attractive; pleasing to the senses or mind

Beau! You're beautiful!

Thanks.

Big Elephants Are Usually beautiful

because *conjunction* - for the reason that

Big elephants can always understand small elephants

I know exactly what you mean.

before *preposition, conjunction, adverb* - prior to; in preparation for; in front of

*Don't forget the **e** before it's too late!*

beginning
noun - the first part, or the start of something; origin

Think about an *inn* hidden in the word beginning:

In the begi<u>nn</u>ing,
*I go to the **inn***

believe
verb - think that something is true or real

Amazingly, the word <u>lie</u> is placed in the middle of believe.

It cures all ailments!

Don't be<u>lie</u>ve a lie!

ailment = illness

benefit
noun - an advantage or profit gained; a helpful or good effect

Try to think of a way to remember the *e* between *ben-* and *-fit*

<u>Ben</u>, '**<u>e</u>** is very **<u>fit</u>**!

between
preposition, adverb - in the space that separates two places or things

Remember there are three *e's* in between.

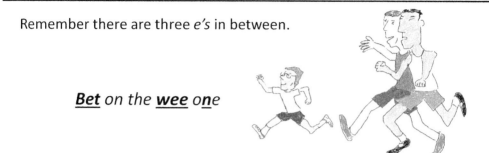

Bet on the **wee** o**n**e

bizarre
adjective - very strange and unusual; peculiar

Remember there is only one *z* and two *r's*

What are you reading?

Shakespeare

*It is bizarre and **z**any that **a**ll **r**hinos **r**ead **e**verything*

bruise
noun - an injury appearing as a discoloured mark on the skin; *verb* - to develop a bruise, or to cause someone to have a bruise

A tricky word where the *-ui* sounds like -oo, and has a silent *e* at the end – this also happens with *cruise*. Try using a sentence like this

***B**rian **r**ubbed **U**ncle **I**an's **s**ore **e**lbow*

business *noun* - the activity of buying and selling goods or services; a particular company doing business; matters that relate to a person

*There's a **bus** **in** every **s**uccess **s**tory*

calendar *noun* - a document that shows the days, weeks, and months of a year; a list of events and dates that are important to note

Try to remember that calendar ends with *-dar* not *-der*!

Dar**a checked the calen**dar

careful *adjective* - paying attention to avoid a mistake or accident

The common mistake is to add an extra *l* to make it *full*.

*Be **careful** **not** to make it **full***

In fact, for all adjectives, remember to spell the ending as **-ful** and not with two l's.

(See page 95 for more on -ful)

careless *adjective* - not taking care or giving sufficient attention to avoid harm or error

care • less

Less is more – don't be care<u>less</u>

category *noun* - a class or division of things, or people regarded as having similar characteristics

The **<u>cat</u> <u>e</u>**ats **<u>gory</u>** stuff

(gory = gruesome, unpleasant)

caught *verb* - past tense of catch; took possession of something

*You (**<u>U</u>**) are c<u>au</u>ght between the **<u>A</u>**rmy and the **<u>G</u>**uards*

ceiling
noun - the upper interior surface of a room; a top limit set on prices, wages, or spending; the maximum height an aircraft can reach

*See (**C**) the **e**levated **i**lluminations on the ceiling*

cemetery
noun - a place where the dead are buried

Remember there are three *e's* but no *a's* in *cemetery*

or

*There are no **a**'s in the cemetery*

The ghosts say, 'E, E, E' (cemetery)

chaos
noun - complete disorder and confusion

Cyclones, **h**urricanes **a**nd **o**ther **s**torms

chauffeur *noun* - a person hired to drive a car or vehicle

Chauffeurs drive Fancy Friends and you (u) too! (2 u's)

chocolate *noun* - a sweet, normally brown food made from cacao seeds, used in many desserts

Choco • late
Don't be late
for chocolate

choice *noun* - an act of selecting an option; the range or variety of things from which you can choose

*On **Ice**, I made a choice to*
find my voice and rejoice

> **choir** *noun* - a group of people who sing together

Think of a choir of Chimpanzees and Orangutans.

Chimpanzees & **o**rangutans **i**n **r**hythm

> **chose** *verb* - past tense of choose; has selected, made a choice

Drop an *o* from choose to get ch**o**se.

Charles *chose*
the **c**oiled **hose**

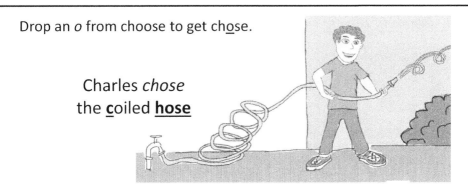

Coiled = a connected series of spirals or loops

> **church** *noun* - a building for Christian religious activities

Think of being surrounded by *ch* on either side

__UR__ (You are) in a ch__ur__ch

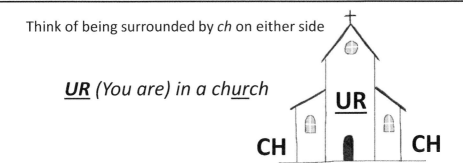

collision *noun* - an accident where two moving objects hit each other; a conflict between opposing ideas

Think of two *l*'s coming together

*Two Learners (LL) will co**ll**ide
if not careful*

column *noun* - an upright pillar that usually supports a structure; a vertical division of a page or text

Here you need to remember the silent *n*.

*Think of a **man** on top of a tall colu**mn***

Is that you, Carl?

committee *noun* - a group appointed to represent a larger group of people to make decisions or collect information, research something

Try to remember the three sets of double letters (*m, t, e*) in committee:

*Two monkeys (**MM**), two tigers (**TT**), and two elephants (**EE**)
were on the **committee***

compliment *noun* - an expression of praise or admiration; *verb* - to praise or admiration for someone

Well done! Bravo!

*A **compliment** puts you in the **lime**light*

concede *verb* - to admit that something is true; to accept defeat; to give away something

Focus on the word **once**, which is hidden within:

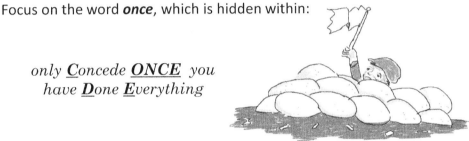

*only **C**oncede **ONCE** you have **D**one **E**verything*

conscience *noun* - a sense of personal belief in what is right and wrong, which guides ones behaviour and actions

Conveniently, if you remember how to spell science, then conscience should be somewhat easy:

*Use **SCIENCE** when spelling **CONSCIENCE***

correspond *verb* - have a close similarity, match or be equal; to communicate by writing

Remember there are two *r's* in *correspond*:

*To co**rr**espond there must be two **r**eplies (2-r's)*

could *verb*
past tense of can; used to ask permission; used to indicate a possibility

should *verb*
used to describe what is correct, an obligation or duty; used to say what is probable

would *verb*
past tense of will; used to show a possibility, a request, willingness or desire

All three can be remembered using **OULD** – "**O**h **U** **L**ucky **D**uck"

Oh, you lucky duck!

Must have won the lottery.

counterfeit *noun* - an exact copy of something for usually dishonest purposes; *adjective* something made to appear genuine, with usually bad intent; *verb* imitate something fraudulently

The difficult part is the *e* – showing up where it seems it should not. Try remembering the *-feit*:

Counter**feit** –
Fakes **E**xposed **I**n **T**ime

courtesy *noun* - polite behaviour or action

Court • esy
He showed her a <u>court</u>*esy on the* **<u>court</u>**

criticise *verb* - express disapproval, point out the faults of something; give an opinion on something

Remember there is a **CRITIC** *in* <u>criti</u>*cise*

Sorry, it's just not good enough

crucial *adjective* - of extreme importance; key to the success of something

Remember the *u* and *c*

*Crucial **r**ules **u**pset **c**rocodiles **i**n **a** lagoon*

cupboard *noun* - a cabinet with doors used for storage

The difficult part is usually to remember the *p*

*Put the **CUP**s in the cupboard*

curiosity *noun* - an interest to know or learn about something; something that is interesting because it is rare or unusual

There is a loss of the second *u* from the adjective *curious*.

Bitcoin is looking a good buy this year

*Cats **u**sually **r**each interesting **o**pinions sitting **i**n **t**he **y**ard*

* Never take investment advice from a cat

deceased adjective - dead

dec • eased

In **Dec**ember the pain **eased**

deceive verb - to hide the truth

Deceive does follow the 'i before e except after c' rule, but you need to remember that there is an **ei** combination in *deceive*:

*Ellie's Intuition told her she was being **dece̲ived***

definite adjective - something that is certain; noun - something that is certain to happen

Remember there are two i's in definite

de • fin • ite

I must think twice (two i's) to be definite

description *noun* – a written or spoken statement about a person, thing or event, that tells you what it is like

Focus on the word is *script*:

de **script** ion

What did you think of my script?

It defies description

desert *noun* - a sandy area without much rain

dessert *noun* - a sweet dish served at the end of the main meal

Desert or dessert? Keep these rules in mind:

A desert is pretty empty – only one S

A dessert is Sweet Stuff – and plenty of it

destroy *verb* - to damage something so that it cannot be used; completely defeat; ruin someone emotionally

The key to remember this spelling is to use an *e*

Enemies destroy

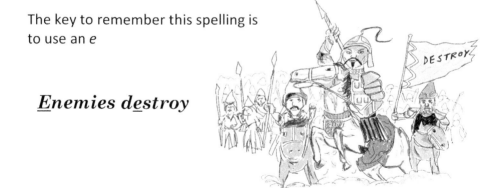

difficulty
noun - a problem; not easy to understand or to do

Sometimes saying the letters aloud can be a good memory tip. Here is a phrase that may be helpful:

(Say Aloud) 'Mrs. **D**, Mrs. **I**, Mrs. **FFI**, Mrs. **C**, Mrs. **U**, Mrs. **LTY**'

disappear
verb - be lost or go missing; cease to exist

With the word *appearance*, we focused on the two *p's* (pea, pear). Now think of the two *p's* and one *s*:

*The **p**ea and the **p**ear disappeared from the **s**tage*

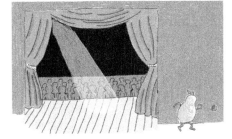

disappointed
adjective - sad or upset because something did not happen that was wanted

*Sally was disappointed that only **one S**eal and **two P**enguins could make it to her birthday party*

Remember that there is only one *s* and two *p's* in *disappointed*

31

disastrous
adjective - extremely bad; causing great damage

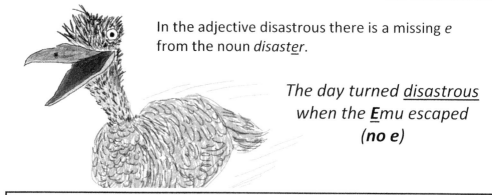

In the adjective disastrous there is a missing *e* from the noun *disast<u>e</u>r*.

The day turned <u>disastrous</u> when the <u>E</u>mu escaped
(no e)

discipline
noun - the ability to control yourself according to strict rules; a particular area of study, especially at a university

Think of the word disc to help remember the correct spelling.

That really takes **discipline**!

*The **<u>disc</u> <u>I</u> p**layed was on the **<u>line</u>***

discuss
verb - talk about a subject with someone

We can use the word disc again with discuss, and remember to include the extra *s* at the end:

*He discussed the **<u>disc</u>** with **<u>U</u>**ma, **<u>S</u>**teve, and **<u>S</u>**am*

does *verb* - third person singular of do

Remember the *e* in *does*.

*Does the **doe** **s**ing?*

doubt *noun* - a feeling of uncertainty, or hesitation; *verb* - feel uncertain about something

*Be (**b**) in dou**b**t*

Which ones are the Marigolds?

*The **b**ee was in **doubt** about which flowers he liked, and those he did not*

dreamt *verb* - past tense of dream; have experienced dreams

This spelling is included because it is the only word in English that ends in -*mt*.

*Dreams and **m**ore **t**rances (MT)*

eccentric *adjective* - uncommon, abnormal , strange; *noun* - a person with uncommon and strange behaviour

Eccentric Carl gave a Cent to Ric

Don't spend it all at once!

economic *adjective* - relating to trade, industry and money; likely to make a profit

The best approach to spelling this word is to break it down in the syllables:

e • co • nom • ic

But there's no microphone.

Well, then go **eco**, **no mic**!

Egypt *noun* - a country in Northern Africa

Every Goat Yells 'Party Time!' in Egypt

eight *number* - the number 8

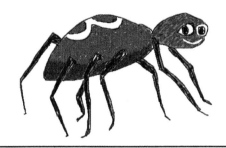

Eight Is Great - Hope you can Tolerate (so many legs!)

embarrass *verb* - cause someone to feel self-conscious, nervous, or uncomfortable

Remember the two *r's* and two *s's* in *embarrass*:

*Do you get **R**eally **R**ed **A**nd **S**mile **S**hyly?*

emphasis *noun* - a special importance to something in speaking or writing

Here we want to remember to use the *ph* for the *f*-sound, and the *a* for the *uh*-sound.

*The **em**peror **ph**oned **a** **sis**ter*

35

enough *pronoun* - as much or as many is needed; *adverb* - to the necessary degree or extent

*Emma, **no** – **u** (you'll) **g**et **h**urt! **Enough** of that!*

environment *noun* - the air, water, and land in and on which people or animals live

IRON MEN *Train in any envi<u>ronmen</u>t*

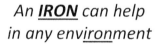

*An **IRON** can help in any envi<u>ron</u>ment*

or

equipped *adjective* - having the necessary items for a task

Here it is good to remember that this word has two *p's*:

*It is important to be **equipped** for a **p**articular **p**urpose*

Did you remember the popcorn?

especially *adverb* - more than usual, or more than other things; for a specific reason

Remember the two *l*'s when you think of ally (as with accidentally):

*It is <u>e</u>specially important to help your <u>**special**</u> <u>**ally**</u>*

essential *adjective* - extremely important; *noun* a thing that is extremely important

The two *s*'s are the key, or shall we say, **essential**?

<u>S</u>turdy <u>s</u>ails are e<u>ss</u>ential

exaggerate *verb* - represent something as larger, more important, better or worse than it actually is

Remember that beside the two *g*'s, the *-ate* ending.

The <u>g</u>igantic <u>g</u>iraffe liked to <u>exaggerate</u> about the <u>e</u>xtra <u>r</u>ice he <u>ate</u>.

First, I had the Basmati, then the Pilau, but the long-grain was my favourite

excellent *adjective* - outstanding, superb

Remember there are two *l's* .
Think of the word cell:

The ex**cell**ent wizard sat
in his **cell.**

exercise *noun* - an activity done to improve physical health; an activity done for a specific purpose; *verb* use or apply; to engage in physical activity

Remember the ending *-cise*:

***Exercise* *c*an *i*mprove *s*trength and *e*nergy**

existence *noun* - the state of being real; a way of life

Keep in mind there are three *e's* in *exist<u>e</u>nce*:

<u>E</u>veryone's <u>E</u>xist<u>e</u>nce is <u>E</u>ssential

extremely *adverb* - very

Don't forget the final *e*

Extreme + ly

***Extreme** *e**lephants are extrem**e**ly rare*

faithfully *adverb* - in a loyal manner; in a factual or true way

This is a word where we do need the two l's in full.

*Every year Santa faith**full**y ensures the stockings are **full** of presents*

familiar *adjective* - well known because of having met, seen or heard before; in a close relationship

Try to remember there is only one *l*, by using the word ***liar*** that ends the spelling of familiar:

That **liar** looks fami**liar**

I don't be**lie**ve him

39

famous *adjective* - known and recognized by many people

Think of using *mouse* at the end without an *e*:

The famous
mouse lost an E

fascinate *verb* - attract the attention and strong interest of someone

The key to spelling fascinate is to remember the *sc* combination, similar to science:

Are you
fascinated with
science?

February *noun* - the second month of the year

feb • ru • ary
Frosts, **e**ven **b**lizzards **r**each **u**s **a**nd **r**un **y**early

fiery *adjective* - having a bright red colour; burning strongly and brightly; showing very strong feelings; spicy (food)

This would be an easier word to spell if the *r* and *e* were not reversing positions from *fire*.

__E__ating __R__ed chilies can be fi__er__y

foreign *adjective* - belonging to or from a country not your own; strange and unfamiliar, not belonging to something

Here is another exception to the 'i before e' rule. Focus on the beginning of the word by using this aid with *before*:

Be__fore__ __I__ __g__o to foreign __n__ations, I always check my passport

forty *number* - the number 40

How many candles, Mama?

Remember to drop the *u* from *four* when going to forty

You (u) forget when you're 40

41

generally *adverb* - usually, most of the time; broadly speaking

Try and focus on the two *l*'s by thinking of the word rally:

*The general liked going to the **rally***

giraffe *noun* - a tall mammal with a patterned coat and a long neck

Two long-necked ff's make a giraffe

g i r a ff e

government *noun* - the people with authority to make laws and policies of a country, or region; the system of making and applying laws

Wear this instead, Your Majesty

To ***govern me**ant* he would have to remove the A

grammar
noun - the system of rules and structure of a language

Remember the two *m's* as well as to end with *ar* and <u>not</u> *er.*

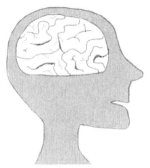

You don't have to be a <u>**m**</u>*aster* <u>**m**</u>*ind to go* <u>**far**</u> *with good gramm* <u>**ar**</u>

grateful
adjective - showing or expressing appreciation to someone

Remember this starts with *grate,* <u>not</u> great.

Dan was <u>grate</u>*ful for* **grate**d *cheese*

guarantee
noun - a formal promise; a warranty; *verb* make a formal assurance of certain conditions; to promise with certainty

Remember both the -ua and two e's

The <u>**guar**</u>*dian* <u>**ant**</u> <u>**tee**</u>*s off*

handkerchief *noun* - a small square cloth used for wiping the nose or eyes

Remember the d in *handkerchief*.

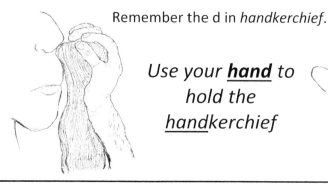

*Use your **hand** to hold the handkerchief*

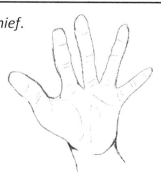

harass *verb* - annoy or upset someone

Remember the single *r* on this one.

*The fly **harass**ed the ragged donkey*

height *noun* - the distance from the top to the bottom of something; the distance of something measured above a surface

weight *noun* - the heaviness of something expressed as a measure; an object that is heavy

Try to remember these together as they are both measurements and have the word *eight* contained within:

*The **height** and **weight** total eight!*

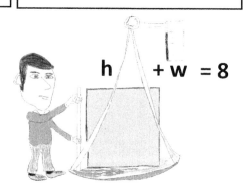

h + w = 8

heroes
noun - (plural of hero) someone who is admired for their bravery or their achievements

__E__xplorers and __S__portspeople are some of our hero__es__

Hero__es__ are __e__xtra __s__pecial

humorous
adjective - funny

The *u* changes position from humo__ur__ to humoro__us__:

You (__u__) are humoro__us__ only at the end

It was humoro__us__ to __us__

immediately
adverb - now, at once, without pause; close to something in distance or time

Keep in mind the two *m's* and the *-ate* ending.

The __m__ad __m__onkey __ate__ the sandwich __immediate__ly

independent *adjective* - not influenced or controlled by an outside authority; not taking any financial or other assistance

The trick is to remember the three *e's*

*The **e**lephant's **pen** made a **dent** in the giraffe's present*

innocent *adjective* - not guilty of a crime; not responsible or involved in an event; *noun* - a pure or naïve person

***In no cent**ury is murder innocent*

intelligent *adjective* - clever, smart

***In tell**ing, the **gent** showed he was intelligent*

interrupt
verb - stop the progress of a conversation, activity, or process for a short period

Remember there are two *r's* in interrupt:

*It is **r**eally **r**ude to interrupt*

irritable
adjective - easily annoyed

Don't forget the two *r's*

*Arrgh! (**R**) Missing an **R** is ir**r**itable*

island
noun - an area of land surrounded completely by water

Is that **land**?

jewellery *noun* - decorative items that are worn, such as necklaces, rings, and bracelets

***Elle** really loves jew<u>elle</u>ry*

language *noun* - a communications system of speaking and writing

*<u>**U**</u> (you) should really learn a language at your **age***

laugh *noun* - a sound made to show you are happy or have found something funny

<u>L</u>augh <u>a</u>nd you'll (<u>u</u>) <u>g</u>et <u>h</u>appy!

league *noun* - a group of teams playing a particular sport, who compete with each other; a group of people or countries who join together for a specific purpose

The Premier <u>League</u> <u>l</u>ets <u>e</u>ager <u>a</u>dults <u>g</u>et <u>u</u>nusually <u>e</u>xcited

leisure *noun* - time when you are not working; the use of free time to do things that are enjoyable

<u>L</u>ions <u>e</u>at <u>i</u>mmense <u>s</u>teaks at <u>leis</u>ure

length *noun* - the measurement of an object from one end to the other; the amount of time something lasts

Increase the len<u>g</u>th with <u>G</u>

liaise *verb* - cooperate with another group on a subject of mutual concern; to act as a link between two different groups or people

Try to remember the two *i's* on either side of the *a*:

Isabelle **and** *Ivy must liaise*

library *noun* - a building or room containing a collection of books, periodicals, and other materials, for use by the public or members

Remember the two *r's* by focusing on *rar*:

*You can find **rar**e books in the lib**rar**y*

lightning *noun* - the natural electrical discharge between a cloud and the ground, usually with a bright flash of light during a storm

Don't put an *e* in lightning!

*Everyone **e**scaped from the lightning (**no E**)*

lion *noun* - a large cat found in Africa and north-western India

***L**ions **i**ntimidate **o**thers **n**icely*

llama *noun* - a domesticated pack animal, valued for its fleece

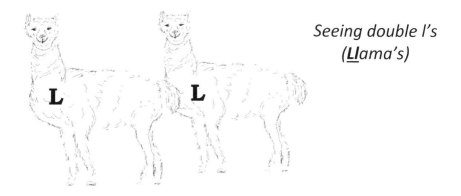

Seeing double l's
*(**Ll**ama's)*

lollipop *noun* - a boiled sweet attached to the end of a stick

Remember there are three *l's*

*I **l**ove **l**iquorice*
*l**oll**ipops*

maintenance *noun -* the process or work required to keep something in good condition; financial support for someone's living expenses

*The **main** work was done by **ten** ants (**ance**)*

manoeuvre *noun -* a movement that requires skill to complete; a military exercise; *verb -* move carefully or guide something

*Standing a **man** **o**n **e**very **u**mbrella (is a) **v**ery **r**are **e**vent*

marvellous *adjective* - amazing, extraordinary

Remember to use two *l*'s

<u>l</u>adybirds and <u>l</u>eopards have marve<u>ll</u>ous spots

mathematics *noun* - the study of numbers, shapes and space

*He sat on **the mat** for Ma<u>the mat</u>ics*

meagre *adjective* - a very small amount that is not enough

*<u>**Me agre**</u>es – that's meagre*

measure *verb* - find out the exact amount or size of something; judge; *noun* - a way of achieving something; a size or amount of something

That seems like a lot!

*Be **sure** your mea**sure** is correct before you start*

---

medallion *noun* - a metal disc worn on a chain or string around the neck; a small round cut of meat with no bones

*They gave the **medal** to the **lion***

---

medieval *adjective* - relating to the Middle Ages (approx. AD 600 – 1500)

Next time, don't eat all the cookies!

Remember the *-val* ending instead of *–vil*

Also keep in mind the word *die* in the middle of me<u>die</u>val

*Medi**eval** people may have been brutal, but that didn't make them **evil***

millennium *noun* - one thousand years

There are two *l's* and two *n's* in *millennium*

1   250   500   750   1000

1000 years last long and need numbering

---

miniature *adjective* - describing a small copy of something;
noun - a very small copy of something

*There's a **mini** '**a**'*
hidden in the
miniature town

(can you find it?)

---

minimum *noun* - the smallest amount necessary or possible;
adjective - describing the smallest amount required or possible

To keep mistakes to a minimum, I
*like to take my **Mini Mum** with me*
from time to time.

Don't forget your homework!

mischievous
adjective - describing behaviour that causes trouble but is not meant to be harmful

<u>Mis</u>erable **<u>Ch</u>**arles **<u>i</u>**nserted **<u>e</u>**xtra **<u>v</u>**egetables **<u>o</u>n <u>us</u>**

muscle
noun - tissue in a human or animal body that can contract, in order to produce movement

Focus on the *CL* in muscle

<u>cl</u>imbing improves mus**<u>cl</u>**es

mysterious
adjective - unexplainable; not known; strange

<u>My</u> <u>s</u>ecret <u>t</u>reasure <u>mys</u>teriously disappeared

naïve *adjective* - showing lack of experience, wisdom or judgement; too willing to believe someone is telling the truth; innocent

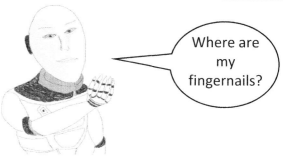

Artificial Intelligence can be naïve sometimes

Where are my fingernails?

Note: The double dot over the *i* in naïve is called a **dieresis**. This means the *a* and *i* have their own separate sounds

necessary *adjective* - needed for a particular purpose

THE **NECESSARY** BRAND
COMFORTABLE • SIMPLE • STYLISH

It is necessary for a shirt have one collar and two sleeves

niece *noun* - a daughter of one's brother or sister, or a daughter of one's wife/husband's brother or sister

My niece is extremely careful with elephants

noticeable *adjective* - easily seen, or recognised

*It is notic<u>e</u>able if you forget the **E***

novel *noun* - a long written story with imaginary characters or events; *adjective* - new or unusual

<u>N</u>ovels <u>o</u>ffer <u>v</u>ery <u>e</u>xciting <u>l</u>anguage

occasion *noun* - referring to a particular time or event; a special event; *verb* - to cause something

For a special o<u>cc</u>asion – travel over two seas (two <u>c</u>'s)

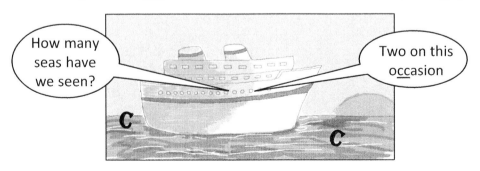

occur *verb* - happen; exist

See (**C**) it o**cc**urs twice!

ocean *noun* - a very large area of sea (the five Oceans: Atlantic, Pacific, Indian, Arctic, Antarctic)

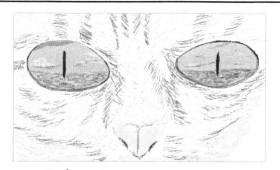

Only **c**ats **e**yes **a**re **n**arrow

often *adverb* - frequently

I heard it played ***ten*** times – that's of**ten**

omission
noun - something left out or not included

Remember omission has only **one** *m* and **two** *s's*:

SCENE 1   SCENE 2

*The story had one **m**iddle but didn't omit two **s**cary **s**cenes*

---

parallel
adjective - lines that are side by side and have the same distance between them

Parallel has **parallel lines** in the middle and one *l* at the end

$$\text{para} \cdot \textbf{ll} \cdot \text{el}$$

---

parliament
noun - a group of people who are elected to make laws for a country

Remember the *i* in the middle of parliament by focusing on *I am*

__I am__ in the parli__am__ent

60

particularly *adverb* - more than usual; giving a special emphasis

*This is the **part I** see you (**CU**) like*

To the park, please!

pastime *noun* - something done for enjoyment rather than work

*As his favourite pastime, he liked to walk **past** the l**ime** .*

It's sublime!

piece *noun* - a portion, or section of something; an artistic creation; *verb* - assemble something from parts

peace *noun* - calm and quiet; a period of time without war

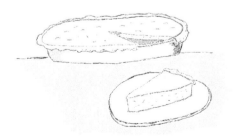

A **pie**ce of **pie**

Give **pea**s (peace) a chance

people *noun* - collective term for humans; members of a particular country or group

*P*eople *e*at *o*ther *p*eople's *l*eftovers *e*very day

permanent *adjective* - intended to last indefinitely; *noun* - a type of hair treatment that lasts for a few weeks

The horse's <u>mane</u> was per**mane**nt

perseverance *noun* - determination to finish a job or achieve a goal despite difficulty and hardship

*Pers*ons *ever*
(at the)
d*ance*

persuade
verb - convince someone to do something by using reason or argument

*You (**u**) must pers**u**ade them*

JOB INTERVIEWS →

pharaoh
noun - a ruler in ancient Egypt

__P__lease __h__ear __a__bout __o__ur __r__ulers __a__nd __o__ther __h__eroes

piano
noun - a large musical instrument with a keyboard

__P__lay __i__n __a__ __n__oisy __o__rchestra

pigeon *noun* - type of bird with a small head and typically grey and white feathers

*The pigeon saw a **pig** **e**ntering*

pleasant *adjective* - enjoyable, nice

*Please (the) **ant***

poison *noun* - a substance that causes severe illness or death; *verb* - to give poison to someone or an animal

Do you have any Hemlock?

potion = a liquid with special abilities

*The **Po**(tion) **is on** the list*

possession *noun* - the fact of having, owning or controlling something; an article or something that is owned

Remember the four *s's* in po<u>ss</u>e<u>ss</u>ion

Silver Swans and Sapphire Stones – that's a lot of po<u>ss</u>e<u>ss</u>ions!

practice *noun* - exercise repeated to gain or improve a skill; a habit or custom; a job or business that requires a lot of training and skill

practise *verb* - perform an activity regularly in order to gain or improve skills; carry out an activity on a regular basis

Think of *ice*:

Ends in *ise*:

*The nurse put **ice** on it in the doctor's pract**ice***

*Pract**ise** t**o** **i**mprove **s**ports **e**xcellence*

pray *verb* - to speak to a god or another deity to express love, thanks or to ask for something

prey *noun* - an animal that is hunted and killed for food by another animal

Angels pray

Eagles prey

principal *adjective* - the most important, main; *noun* - the most important person in an organization

principle *noun* an idea or belief that is the basis for making decisions or a system of belief; a scientific theory

*The prince is not your **pal***

*principle ends with **le** just like ru**le**.*

pronunciation *noun* how a word sounds when spoken

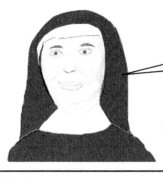

It's easy to spell pro**nun**ciation when you think of the nun

*The **nun** has good pron<u>un</u>ciation*

quay *noun* - area where goods are loaded onto ships

Quay begins with *qu-* but sounds like *key*

*Join the **qu**eue tod**ay** to get the key*

queue *noun* - a line of people, waiting to enter, be served, or to buy something; *verb* - wait in a queue

What are we waiting for?

<u>Q</u>ueens <u>u</u>sually <u>e</u>at <u>up</u> <u>e</u>verything (as they don't have to <u>queue</u>).

Also, imagine u's and e's lining up

67

receive *verb* - get something (an object, an emotion, a message), or be given something

*It is better to g**ive** than to rece**ive***

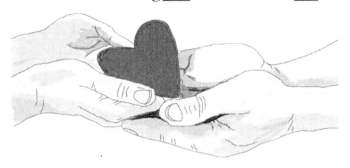

recognise *verb* - identify something or someone from having known them from before; accept the existence or truth of something

Remember the *-ise* ending

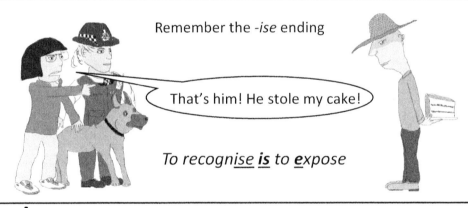

That's him! He stole my cake!

*To recogn**ise** **is** to **e**xpose*

reign *verb* - rule as a monarch (King, Queen, Emperor, etc.); *noun* - the period of rule of a monarch

***R**oyals **e**njoy **i**nviting **g**reat (k)**n**ights*

reindeer

noun - a type of deer with large antlers

Remember there is an *e* where you might expect an *a* in reindeer:

*Its not raining (no a) dear, the r**ei**nd**ee**r can b**e** at **e**as**e** (3 e's)*

restaurant

noun - a place where you can sit down and pay for a meal

*I'll **rest** **a**nd you (**u**) **rant***

Why don't you have Marshmallow pie? And what about Prune juice? I need to have some options... This is ridiculous!

rant = talk loudly or angrily at length about something

rhyme

verb use words that have a same last syllable sound; *noun* - a word that has a same last sounding syllable as another word; a poem

Remember that the *hy* has the same sound as in the word *why:*

Let's run away to a lovely little cafe We'll laugh all day Come what may

Having a ball, sitting here on the wall

*W**hy** r**hy**me all the time?*

rhythm *noun* - a strong pattern of sounds or movement repeated in music, poetry or dance; the pattern of change or movements in nature

<u>R</u>hythm <u>h</u>elps <u>y</u>our <u>t</u>wo <u>h</u>ips <u>m</u>ove

ridiculous *adjective* - laughable, absurd

It's ridiculous to see you (<u>cu</u>) <u>l</u>aying <u>o</u>ver <u>u</u>ncooked <u>s</u>ausages

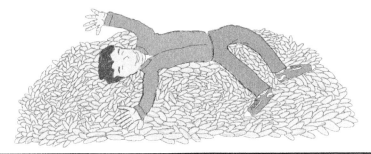

roofs *noun* - (plural of roof) the top covering of a building or other structure housing people

The <u>r</u>oofs <u>o</u>n <u>o</u>ld <u>f</u>lats <u>s</u>ag.

I've got to get that fixed soon.

sandal *noun* - a type of open shoe held together with straps

Only one *l* in *sandal*

*Sam **and** Alice wore sandals*

---

scene *noun* - a place where something has happened or happens in a story, or in real life; a segment of a story, movie or play

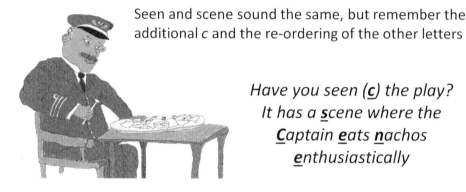

Seen and scene sound the same, but remember the additional *c* and the re-ordering of the other letters

*Have you seen (**c**) the play? It has a **s**cene where the **C**aptain **e**ats **n**achos **e**nthusiastically*

---

schedule *noun* - a timetable of events; *verb* - arrange or plan an event; include something in a timetable of events

*As a r**ule**, I sche**dule** my afternoons at **sch**ool with the m**ule***

scissors *noun* - a tool used for cutting paper and other materials

Try to remember the middle *s's* in scissors

$\underline{S}$cissors $\underline{c}$ut $\underline{i}$n $\underline{s}$imple $\underline{s}$lices

---

seize *verb* - grab, take hold of something

Focus on the *-ize* ending:

Emma se$\underline{ize}$d the pr$\underline{ize}$

---

sensible *adjective* - realistic, using common sense

Remember to use an *i* in sensible:

***Sibl**ings can be sens$\underline{ible}$*

separate *adjective* - different, distinct; *verb* - move apart, divide

Remember to **separate** the two *a's*:

or

Andy and **A**lex must be
sep**a**r**a**ted

There's **a rat** in
sep**arate**

---

siege *noun* - an attack using military forces to take a city or fortress

Soldiers **i**nvaded **e**very **g**round **e**verywhere

---

skilful *adjective* - possessing skill, talented

Remember to drop one *l*
from the word *skill*:

*Be skilful as you
separate the two **l**'s*

special *adjective* - exceptional, outstanding; specific to a person or place; *noun* - a program for television or broadcast for a particular occasion

*The Special Agent was from the **CIA***

CIA = Central Intelligence Agency (American agency that collects secret information)

---

stationery *noun* - paper, envelopes and writing instruments used to write letters or cards

stationary *adjective* - fixed in one position, not moving

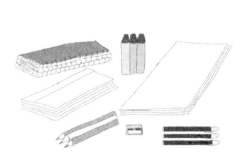

STATIONERY and envelopes are effective for writing letters

STATIONARY is an Adjective STATIONARY is Always there

stomach *noun* - an organ in the body where food is digested

<u>Ch</u>eese gives me stom<u>ach</u> <u>ach</u>es

stopping *participle* - (stop) to end or conclude

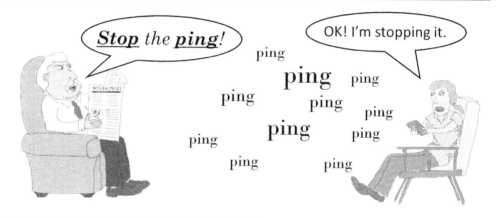

<u>Stop</u> the <u>ping</u>!

OK! I'm stopping it.

ping ping ping ping ping ping ping ping ping ping ping ping

subtle *adjective* - not obvious, small but important; done in an indirect or tactful way in order to achieve something

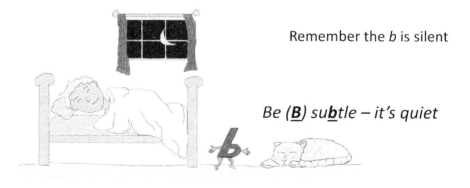

Remember the *b* is silent

Be (<u>B</u>) su<u>b</u>tle – it's quiet

success *noun* the achievement of a goal or aim; a victory

Remember the two *c's* and two *s's*

Courage in climbing spells success

sufficient *adjective* - enough

What **if**... we doubled the ***i's*** and the ***f's***?

*Double the **f***'s and ***i***'s to be su**ffi**c**i**ent*

suggest *verb* - propose an idea; indicate or show something

Don't forget the two *g's* in suggest:

Girl guides make good suggestions

symbol *noun* - a sign or letter used to represent something; a person or thing that represents or stands for something else

| 1 | 2 | 3 | 4 |

*A symbol is a **s**ign **y**ou **m**ake **b**ased **o**n **l**anguage*

| 5 | 6 | 7 | 8 |

Bonus: Can you identify these symbols?
(See page 97 for the answers)

tattoo *noun* - a permanent ink marking in the skin; a military show, with music and marching; a call to soldiers to return in the evening

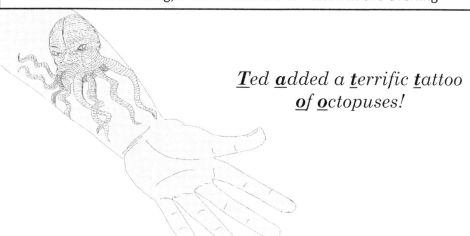

__T__ed __a__dded a __t__errific __t__attoo of __o__ctopuses!

their *determiner* - belonging to someone previously mentioned	**there** *adverb* - in, at or to a location

Their is possessive

There is usually a place

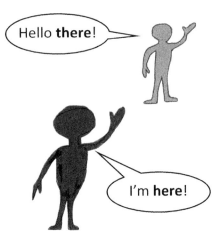

He is the **heir** to t<u>heir</u> fortune

Here is the opposite of t<u>here</u>

> **Also don't forget**
> They're = They are

thorough *adjective* – detailed and careful; complete; done with great care

That's every nail hammered! What's next?

Thor was r**ough** and **thorough**

78

together *adverb* - with each other; in unison

__Get__ __her__ - you'll be to__get__her

tomorrow *noun* - the day after today; *adverb* - on the day after today

Remember the double *r* like in bo**rr**ow and a**rr**ow

Are you ready for tomorrow?

Yes, but I might need some more arrows

Tomo__rr__ow __r__equires __r__eadiness

tongue *noun* - the organ in the mouth used to taste , swallow and help in speaking; a way or style of speaking

A __tong__ of good smells help you (__u__) __e__at

truly *adverb* - honestly; accurately or correctly

Think of spelling July – no *e's*!

*It is tr**uly**
hot in J**uly***

---

twelfth *number* - the 12th in a sequence

Twelve changes to tw**elf**th

Who's next?
Number twelve!

*The **elf** came after the 11th*

---

twentieth *number* - the 20th in a sequence

The *ty* in twenty changes to **tie** in twentieth

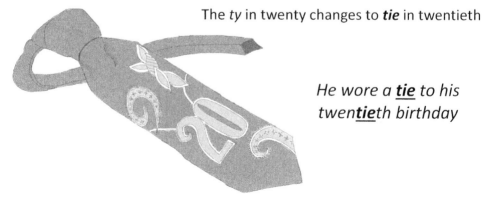

*He wore a **tie** to his
twen**tie**th birthday*

tyranny
noun - oppressive government rule; a situation where there is an unfair use of power

*__T__rust __y__our __Gr__anny, not a **tyranny***

undoubtedly
adverb - certainly

__B__ut __Ted__ will undou__bted__ly win the race

unique
adjective - one of a kind

Are we there yet?

__Uni__nteresting __que__stions are not unique

unnecessary *adjective* - not needed

<u>N</u>auseating <u>n</u>oodles and <u>s</u>kinny <u>s</u>keletons are u<u>nn</u>ece<u>ss</u>ary

Nauseating = sickening

until *preposition, conjunction* - up to (a certain time)

Don't add an extra *l* at the end – until only has one *l* like pencil or lentil:

You can't have any lent<u>il</u>s unt<u>il</u> you write with a penc<u>il</u>

unusual *adjective* - not common, abnormal, surprising

Remember there are
three *u's* in unusual

*It is **unusu**al to
see you (**u**) three
times in one day*

vacuum *noun* - an electrical appliance that cleans floors and surfaces by using suction; a space without gas or matter

Remember there are two *u's* in vacuum:

*Make sure you vac**uu**n **u**nder the **u**pholstery*

vehicle *noun* - a machine used to transport people and other items, usually over land; a medium used to express an idea

Don't forget the *h* in vehicle:

Your car has **hic**-ups!

What's wrong with my ve**hic**le?

HIC

vicious *adjective* - showing a desire to be cruel or physically violent

Don't forget there is a *c* in vicious

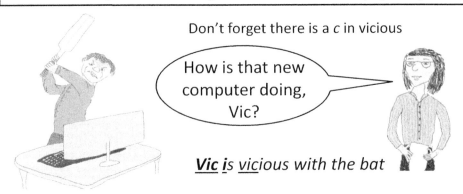

How is that new computer doing, Vic?

***Vic* is *vicious* with the bat**

weather *noun* - the climate in terms of temperature, wind, rain, etc.; *verb* – change by exposure to the climate; successfully deal with a problem	**whether** *conjunction* - if; indicating a choice of alternatives

__We__ (look) __at__ __her__ –
*look at the **weather** lady*

__W__hether __he__ __t__ells __her__
– that is the question

Wednesday *noun* - day of the week coming after Tuesday

Is it Thursday yet?

How about some healthy carrots?

__We__ __d__o __n__ot __e__at __s__weets __day__

weird *adjective* - strange; unnatural

Wacky
elephants **i**n
red **d**resses

Wacky = funny, or amusing in a strange way

welcome *noun, interjection* - a greeting; *verb* - greet in a friendly manner; *adjective* - desirable, pleasing

Great, we can always use more chips!

Only one *l* in welcome

We **l**ike **c**hips **o**n **m**ost **e**venings

yacht *noun* - a medium-sized boat used for racing or recreation

*Yo-yos are cool,
handy, toys
to play on a yacht*

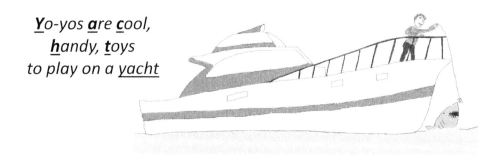

Palindrome Fun

Palindromes are words or phrases that can be spelt the same way backwards (right to left) as normally. Here are some of the more common single word palindromes:

CIVIC	**DAD**	**EVE**
GAG	**GIG**	**KAYAK**
LEVEL	**LOL**	**MADAM**
PEEP	**RACECAR**	**RADAR**
REFER	**REPAPER**	**ROTATOR**
ROTOR	**SOLOS**	**STATS**
TENET	**TOOT**	**WOW**

Palindromes get even more interesting when they are extended to phrases or complete sentences. Here are some particularly funny and interesting ones.

Never odd or even

evil olive

senile felines

gold log

taco cat

Top spot!

Neil, an alien.

A nut for a jar of tuna.

Step on no pets.

No, it is opposition.

Was it a car or a cat I saw?

Dee saw a seed.

Rise to vote, sir.

Mr. Owl ate my metal worm!

Too hot to hoot!

Name now one man.

Ed is on no side.

Madam, I'm Adam.

No lemons, no melon.

Panda had nap.

Nurses run.

Emil saw a slime.

No, it is opposition.

Borrow or rob?

Must sell at tallest sum.

Yawn a more Roman way.

A man, a plan, a canal – Panama

Are we not drawn onward to new era?

Marge lets Norah see Sharon's telegram.

Anne, I vote more cars race Rome to Vienna.

I madam, I made radio! So I dared. Am I mad? Am I?

Cigar? Toss it in a can. It is so tragic.

Some Common Spelling Rules

1) I before E except after C

This may be the only rule that most of us will remember well, perhaps due to the rhyming nature of it. However, despite its popularity, there are some notable exceptions to remember:

Exception: when the EI sounds like a long A, as in 'neighbour' and 'weigh'

More examples: **beige, eight, freight, weight**

Exception: when there is SH sound, as in 'leisure' and 'proficient'

More examples: **ancient, conscience, deficient, efficient**

Even considering the exceptions, there are still more that do not follow this rule, such as **fancies, foreign, forfeit, glaciers, height, policies, society, vein, weird**

2) <u>When there's a Q there's usually a U afterward</u>

Don't **quit** on me now, U!

Oh, be **quiet**!

In spelling words that have a *q*, you can almost always count on using a *u* right after it. They are almost inseparable!

<u>Some examples:</u>

ACQUAINTANCE	CONSEQUENCE
EQUATOR	FREQUENT
LIQUID	MARQUIS
QUARTER	QUESTION
SQUIREL	SUBSEQUENT
TRANQUIL	UNIQUE

<u>Exceptions</u>

qwerty: This is an adjective that describes the standard English type of keyboard design, referring to the letters Q, W, E, R, T, Y being the first six letters from the upper left of the keyboard.

Qiana: A type of nylon used to make shirts and other clothing

Iraq and **Qatar**: countries located in western Asia

Many of the other exceptions are non-English words that are not frequently encountered.

3) Drop the E!

Drop it!

VOWEL SUFFIX ENDING

When adding a **vowel suffix ending** (-able, -ation, -ed, -er, -ing, -ion, -ish, -ous) to a word ending in *e*, you will normally drop the final *e*:

compare +able = comparable
encourage +ing = encouraging
irritate +ion = irritation
use +ing = using

complete +ed = completed
hike +ing = hiking
propose +ing = proposing
write +er = writer

Exception: be
be + ing = being

Exception: If the word ends in -ee, -oe, -ye

canoe +ing = canoeing
see + ing = seeing

dye +able = dyeable

Exception: If the word ends in -ce or -ge, when adding -able or -ous

notice +able = noticeable
salvage +able = salvageable
courage +ous = courageous

Some words you drop the -e and add -ious:

space + ious = spacious   grace + ious = gracious

4) Adding a suffix to words ending in -y

When the word ends in a **vowel** + y, we just add the ending:

bay + s = bays
key + s = keys

betray + ed = betrayed
slay + ing = slaying

> **Exception**
> day + ly = daily

When adding an **-s** to a word ending in a **consonant** + y, drop the y and add **-ies**:

apply > applies
cherry > cherries
fairy > fairies
marry > marries

butterfly > butterflies
fancy > fancies
fly > flies
trophy > trophies

bunny

bunnies

For words that have a **consonant** before the letter **y**, change the y to an i:

beauty + ful = beautiful
empty + ness = emptiness
lazy + ly = lazily

easy + est = easiest
happy + ness = happiness

> ## Going from IE to Y
> In a twist, some words that end in –ie change to a –y when adding -ing:
>
> die > dying   lie > lying   tie > tying

5) Plural spelling of nouns ending in -s, -ss, -z, -ch, -sh, -x

For words ending in -s, -ss, -z, -ch, -sh, and -x, use the plural ending of **-es**

box > boxes

dress > dresses

sandwich > sandwiches

bus > buses

quiz > quizes

wish > wishes

Exception
stomach > stomachs

6) Plural spelling of nouns ending in -f

For some words ending in **f** (also **fe**), we change the **f** to **ves** to make it plural:

calf > calves

loaf > loaves

shelf > shelves

knife > knives

scarf > scarves

A Few Exceptions		
proof > proofs	roof > roofs	chief > chiefs

For words ending in **ff**, we just add **s** to make it plural:

bluff > bluffs

handcuff > handcuffs

cliff > cliffs

sheriff > sheriffs

An Exception
stuff > stuff (already plural)

7) Words Ending in -ful and -fully

We have seen a few of these already as tricky spellings. For **adjectives**, these should always end in **-ful**, not with two L's! Examples include:

beautiful	bashful	careful
cheerful	forceful	powerful
stressful	ungrateful	useful

Only use the spelling *full* when it is on its own.
Here are some examples:

Full Moon   **Full Sail**   **Full English**

When we want to make an **adverb** from these words, we add -ly and now will see **-fully** in the spelling:

beautiful + ly = beautifully   bashful + ly = bashfully
cheerful + ly = cheerfully   forceful + ly = forcefully

Terms Used

- **Noun**: a person, place or thing

- **Pronoun**: a word that refers to a noun

- **Verb**: a word that describes an action

- **Adverb**: a word that modifies a verb, adjective, determiner, preposition, or sentence

- **Adjective**: a word that modifies or describes a noun or pronoun

- **Preposition**: a word used before a noun, noun phrase, or pronoun, connecting it to another word

- **Conjunction**: a word that connects other words, phrases or clauses

- **Interjection**: a word of expression that stands on its own, and expresses a feeling or reaction (ouch!)

- **Determiner**: a word used to note specific or particular things (a, an, the, her, their, those, which)

- **Participle**: a word formed from a verb that is used as an adjective (usually ending in -ed or -ing)

- **Vowel:** a, e, i, o, u

- **Consonant:** any letter that is not a vowel

- **Plural**: more than one

- **Suffix**: a letter or combination of letters added to the end of a word to make a new word

Answers to symbols, pg. 77

1. Thumbs up – everything's good
2. WIFI (Wireless)
3. Hazard/Warning
4. Barber
5. Recycling
6. Euro
7. Peace
8. Infinity

Also available from the Armadillo's Pillow:

The Big 11+ Vocabulary Play Book

- Learn over 1,000 words targeted specifically for Eleven Plus Exam
- 52 successfully tested, engaging activities – includes games, puzzles, cartoons, quizzes, rhymes and tongue twisters that address synonym, antonym, analogy, cloze and category questions in a lively way.
- All the materials are photocopiable

The Big 11+ Logic Puzzle Challenge

- A unique collection of logic puzzles to challenge and prepare children for the Eleven Plus as well as Independent School exams.
- Includes: Non-verbal reasoning, verbal reasoning, riddles and brain teasers, worded problems, spatial reasoning, cube nets, mazes and much more!
- The variety of challenges should stimulate and keep children interested as they improve their ability to solve different types of problems.

The 11+ Vocabulary Word Search Extravaganza

- Word Search book focused exclusively on vocabulary required for Eleven Plus exams
- Organised by synonyms, antonyms, subjects and themes
- Hours of fun whilst learning anywhere
- Increase vocabulary retention and spelling through challenging word search puzzles

Contact us at: thearmadillospillow@gmail.com

Printed in Great Britain
by Amazon

42738702R00061